CANDLE MAGIC

Raven Willow

Ebooks are not transferable. They cannot be sold, shared or given away and doing so is an infringement on the copyright of this work.

Candle Magic
Copyright © 2014 by Raven Willow

All Rights Are Reserved. No part of this book may be used or reproduced in any manner without written permission from the author, except in the case of brief quotations embodied in articles and reviews.

Introduction

This book is a reference guide for simple, but effective, candle spells. There are spells in this book that you can follow, but we will also look at how to put together your own spell to suit your needs. Candle magic can be one of the simplest types of magic to perform. You can cast any kind of spell with only a candle, because the most important ingredient in the entire spell is your own intention. You can enhance your candle magic by inscribing, anointing or dressing your candle and by choosing specific colours to complement your intentions. Those are all excellent ways to enhance your spells and we will look at them all individually. Never forget though, that these are only enhancements. With focus and the right intention you can cast a powerful spell without any of those elements; and even the most carefully chosen enhancements won't make a spell work if you don't focus your intention properly.

So, what is intention? Simply put, your intention is what you aim to achieve from your spell. If your intentions are not specific, you won't get a specific result. If your spell is to enable you to have enough money to buy a new car, focus your intention and the spell on the car. If you focus on just the money, the Goddess may send you surprising and unfortunate results. It's not uncommon for an unfocused spell to work with unintended effects, so you could get just enough money for the car only to find yourself faced with some unexpected bills that prevent you using it to actually buy a car with. Make sure you know exactly what your intention is before you start, and that your heart is in it.

On the subject of hearts, be very careful with love spells. These are one definite area where it is not a good idea to be too specific with your intentions. Specifically intending to control a person's free will so that they fall in love with you is not advisable and breaks the Wiccan Rede, which asks that you don't harm anyone. That said, there's no harm in asking the Goddess to send some love in your direction. By focusing here on generally attracting love to yourself you are simply asking for a helping hand finding a real love, and not trying to wield a magical form of mind control. Not every witch is a Wiccan, but sticking to the principles or the Rede is a good way to make sure that your magic is not blurring any ethical lines regardless of your own faith system.

Whatever you are hoping to achieve with your spell, you will find candle magic is an easy and accessible form of magic that even beginners can quickly become adept at.

Preparation

Candle magic is simple. In a pinch, you can just light your candle, focus your intentions for a while, and let the candle burn down. If you want to get the most out of your spell, however, you should prepare your mind, body, and working space first. It is best to have a particular place to do your spell casting which is private and where you won't be disturbed. Outside is great, weather and nosy neighbours permitting, but anywhere inside that is clean and comfortable will be fine. If you have a permanent working space you can set up an altar using a small table or even a sturdy box, which you can place all of your spell items on. If you don't have an altar, don't worry

If you can, start by taking a warm bath or shower. While you wash away the day's grime, imagine that the water is also washing away all of the day's worries. Close your eyes and imagine that the water is surrounded by a bright aura of light. As it washes over you, imagine you are absorbing the light and it is cleansing you from within, pushing away any doubts, insecurities and worries. When your bath or shower is over, dry yourself gently and if you like, apply a scented body lotion or oil. Aromatherapy oil blends are a good choice, as you can choose one complementary to your spell. A general relaxing oil like lavender would also be beneficial. Dress in loose, clean clothing. Avoid anything tight fitting that might be uncomfortable and distract you during the spell.

Whenever you perform a spell of any kind you should always cast a circle first, for protection. Make sure that you have everything you need with you for the spell before you cast the circle. Find a quiet space where you won't be disturbed to cast the circle. If you already have a preferred method of casting a circle, then you can follow that method. For those who have never cast a circle, or would like a quick and simple method, follow the steps below:

- Close your eyes and imagine a brilliant white light, the size of a tennis ball, from within your centre.
- Take deep, cleansing breaths and breathe slowly in and out until you have a steady and comfortable breathing rhythm.
- Imagine the light slowly growing, expanding outwards until it fills your whole body.
- Open your eyes, whilst still visualising the light and use your index finger to slowly draw a circle that encloses both you and your tools for the spell.
- As you draw the circle, imagine the light flowing from your fingertips, leaving a flat, illuminated circle on the floor when you finish. Imagine the light from the circle extending up and over you, and down and under you, in a sphere, so that you are enclosed in a brilliant ball of light.

- When you can visualise the sphere perfectly, allow the light to fade, leaving behind an invisible wall of protection that is like a magical bubble around you.

This is your circle that will protect your energy whilst you cast the spell. When you are done with the spell, imagine the bubble as sphere of light again, and slowly draw the light back into you, shrinking it back down to tennis ball size before disappearing. Once you are finished, have something to eat and drink to ground yourself again. It doesn't have to be a big meal, something small like an apple or biscuit is fine.

Choosing your candle

There are a few things to consider when choosing your candle. The first one is which type of candle to use. Tea lights are ok, if you are short on time and want a simple spell. Pillar style candles are great for big spells, you can cast the spell with the same candle over several days or a week until it is burned down. Taper or votive candles are also great for spells and are often large enough to inscribe if you wish. If you are short on cash, birthday candles can usually be bought very cheaply in a mixed pack of different colours and are perfectly fine for very simple spells that don't require the same candle to be used to repeat the spell over the course of a few days.

Beeswax candles are often considered the crème de la crème of candles for magic, but they can be more expensive. Stock up on candles in different sizes, shapes, colours and materials when you can find them at a good price, and then choose the most suitable as you need it.

You can buy candles in various shapes, and also special candles designed for magic. These will work well enough if you choose to use them, but I don't find that they add anything 'extra' to the results. If you are good at making things you may like to make your own candles to use for magic, and creating candles in shapes representing your intention is an excellent way to enhance your magic. The difference between shop-bought shaped candles, and ones you make yourself is the effort you put in. The more personalised your spell is to you, the better the results.

The next thing to consider is the colour. You should choose a colour that corresponds with your intentions. If you don't have the 'right' colour available, you can use white candles as a substitute for any colour:

White: Purification, protection, truth, peace, Goddess as maiden, youth
Black: Protection, Goddess as crone, overcoming obstacles, binding
Blue: Inspiration, protection, calm, wisdom, patience
Yellow: Healing, intelligence, memory
Orange: Justice, property, adaptability, legal concerns
Green: Abundance, money, success, growth
Red: Energy, defence, passion, career, strength, Goddess as Mother
Pink: Love, reconciliation, peace, caring
Purple: Psychic ability, influence, progress, meditation
Brown: Friendship, neutrality, balance, grounding
Silver: The Goddess, dispel negativity, the moon, astral energy, intuition
Gold: Healing, prosperity, winning, attraction

Preparing your candle

Before you use your candle, you should always cleanse it first. You can do this by leaving it on a windowsill overnight in the light of a full moon. Alternatively, submerge the candle in a bowl filled with sea salt overnight. Once it is cleansed, ask the Goddess to bless the candle. Use whatever words feel comfortable. It could be an elaborate rhyme or a simple request. I like to use the rhyme below:

Bless this candle for my spell
May my magic turn out well
Let it burn so bright and true
May its light guide my will to you

Once you have blessed the candle, charge it with your intention by holding it in your hands as you visualise your intended outcome- driving your new car, getting your well-deserved promotion, removing negative influences from your life. Then, with a sharp object like the tip of a knife (use your athame – ritual knife- if you have one), a nail, pin or even a pencil, inscribe something that symbolises your intention. This can be the picture of a car, the amount of money you need, runes, or if there is space, a few words like 'get promoted', 'break my addiction' etc. If you happen to be using tea lights or very small candles, write or draw this on a piece of paper which can be placed underneath the candle holder during the ritual.

The next step is to anoint your candle with oils if you have them available. Essential oils will also make the candle release a fragrance which has the added bonus of making your ritual area smell lovely. Bear in mind that oil is flammable and after adding it to your candles you should be extra careful when they are lit. You can anoint it with plain olive oil if you don't have any essential oils available. If you have essential oils available, choose one that complements your intentions. Some commonly available oils and their magical correspondences are listed here:

Bergamot: Attract money, lift mood, reach potential
Clove: Sexual desire, courage, attract money, deflect gossip
Frankincense: Break addiction and compulsion, attract prosperity, overcome obstacles
Jasmine: Attract love, encourage creativity, beauty, psychic dreams
Rose: Promote fidelity, encourage friendship, attract romantic love
Lemon: Confidence, clear thinking, see through illusions
Lavender: Brings peace, promotes healing, relaxes tensions
Sandalwood: Increases psychic ability, promote physical energy
Basil: Attract happiness, increase intuition
Sage: Purification, cleansing, spiritual visions
Rosemary: Enhance: memory, promote mental health, healing, remembrance.

When anointing your candle, apply the oil starting at the middle of the candle, smoothing the oil in an upwards motion. Once the top of the candle is anointed, follow the same steps but smooth the oil in a downward motion. As you anoint, focus fully on the outcome you want from your spell. Don't simply rub the oil in an 'up and down' motion over the whole candle, as this can distort the energy and result in unpredictable results.

As you rub the oil from the middle to the top, say:

I consecrate this candle

As a tool of magic

Blessed Be

As you rub the oil from the middle to the bottom, say:

I charge this candle with power

In the name of the Goddess

So mote it be

Timing

The timing of a spell can enhance its effectiveness. Aspects like the phase of the moon and the day of the week can affect the outcome of your spell. The spells I provide in this book all indicate which moon phase is best to use. As a quick guide:

The new moon is the best time to start something new, attract money, or improve health.

The full moon is the best time to work on personal success, career, love, and marriage.

The waning moon is the best time to rid your life of negative influences and bad situations.

If you absolutely cannot perform the spell at the correct moon phase, the best thing to do is to try and perform it on the day of the week that best complements your goal. If you get a chance to combine the two things, your magic will be all the stronger for it. A quick guide to the days of the week:

Monday:
Healing, intuition, family

Tuesday:
Conflict, courage, physical strength

Wednesday:
Communication, self-improvement, psychic ability

Thursday:

Luck, money, legal matters

Friday:

Fertility, love, pleasure

Saturday:

Change, motivation, banishing

Sunday:

Authority, power, friendship

Spells

This section contains some simple spells that you can cast. The candle colours, suggested oils and other spell enhancements are all suggested. Don't forget that you can use white as a substitute for any candle colour in a pinch, and the 3 key elements of candle magic are the candle, the casting of the circle and your own intentions; if you don't have some of the items listed, the spell can be adapted to just involve those 3 things.

As all of these spells involve candles, and some include burning paper, please be extremely careful and take any necessary precautions to avoid damaging yourself or your property. I use a cast iron cauldron to place any lit paper into, and make sure anything flammable is not too close to it. To prevent damage from dripping wax, or the candle flame, you should always use a suitable holder or candle plate for your candles. A small saucer will do for pillar style candles if you don't have anything especially for this. Make sure that whatever you use is made of suitable non-combustible material and is not likely to fall over whilst holding a lit candle.

Some spells ask that you let the candle burn down. Don't ever leave a burning candle unattended. If you cannot let the candle burn down for any reason, put it out and relight it as soon as possible afterwards until it is burnt down. When you put a candle out, don't blow it. Use a candle snuffer or a spoon to snuff it out.

I have provided suggested chants to use, but if you want to say something different that you feel embodies your intentions better, or is more fitting for your personal situation, then you should use your own words. What you say does not have to rhyme, it just has to be heartfelt.

As you perform the spell, watch for how the candle behaves. Note any of the following while the candle burns:

The candle burns very quickly:

If the candle burns down very fast, this is a sign that the magic is strong and may work quickly. Some witches believe that it can also mean that the effects will not last long, and you may have to repeat the spell after a while.

The candle burns extremely slowly:

If the candle burns down very slowly, this is a sign that it will take some time before you see the results of the spell.

The candle flame dips and flares, over and over:

This can happen if you are in a place where there is a draft. If there is no draft, it can be seen as a sign that the magic might only partially work and could be a slow process.

The candle flame goes out before the candle has burned down:

This can be considered as a sign that the spell will not work, and it is a good idea if this happens to re-examine your real intentions. If the spell you are casting breaks the Rede or is something that deep down you know is not a good idea, it may be best to abandon the spell. If you are clear that your intentions are appropriate, and are sure of the intended outcome, then you can begin the spell again after blessing the candle and re-charging it.

The candle flame sizzles, cracks, pops, or makes other noises:

If the candle sizzles and makes lots of noises, this is a sign that you have spirits trying to communicate or assist you. This is usually a positive thing.

The candle creates a lot of smoke:

A lot of smoke can indicate that someone is working against you, or hindering the outcome of the spell.

Interpreting these signs is known as pyromancy, and is a form of candle divination. We'll look at ceromancy, another form of candle divination a little further along in the book.

Banish Negativity:

To banish your own negative feelings or other people's negativity that is bring you down. You will need:

> **A black candle**
> **Sage or Rosemary oil to anoint the candle**
> **Dried Sage (the kind you can buy from the supermarket)**

Cast your circle and light the candle. Focus on the candle flame and visualise all the negativity that you want to banish as a swirling cloud of black fog in the air around you. As the fog passes over the candle flame it dissipates, leaving clean air behind. As you visualise this, chant:

> *Clear this fog and let me see*
> *Through life's many negativities*
> *Let me shine bright through every day*
> *Despite what trials come my way*
> *So it is, and so mote it be*

Once you feel that the air is clear around you sprinkle a little of the dried sage over the candle. Thank the Goddess in your own words and close your circle. Leave the candle burning until it is has burned down.

Lose Weight:

I recommend this spell only if your starting point is an unhealthy weight, or at the very top of your healthy weight range. If you are going to use this spell to try and take your weight below a healthy range, bear in mind that the Wiccan Rede states that you should 'harm none.' This includes yourself. If you feel like you need to lose weight to become prettier or more popular then please consider the self-esteem spell as an alternative- You are already beautiful, I promise you! For this spell you will need:

> **A purple candle**
> **Frankincense oil to anoint the candle**
> **Waning Moon**
> **A small piece of Bloodstone, Amethyst, the aptly named Apatite, or a piece of jewellery that you wear daily.**

Cleanse whichever object you choose in the light of the full moon overnight before using. This should be convenient as the spell works best at a waning moon. You are linking your reducing body with the reducing size of the visible moon.

Cast your circle and light the candle. Preferably perform the spell in a place where you can actually see the moon. Focus on the candle and visualise your excess weight melting away like the wax on the candle. As you visualise this, hold your crystal or piece of jewellery and chant:

> *Melting candle burning bright*
>
> *Help me control my appetite*
>
> *As the moon wanes in the sky,*
>
> *So my weight wanes before my eyes*
>
> *So it is, and so mote it be*

As you chant, visualise that you are pouring positive energy into the crystal or piece of jewellery. When you feel the time is right, thank the Goddess in your own words and close your circle.

Each evening, relight the candle in view of the moon and visualise your body size reducing in line with the moon. Hold your crystal or piece of jewellery as you do this, and imaging the light from the moon refilling it with positive energy. Spend at least 15 minutes doing this and repeat until the new moon.

During the day, whenever you are tempted to eat something unhealthy, take out the crystal or touch the piece of jewellery and use its positive energy to resist making poor diet choices.

Self Esteem:

This spell is good for boosting self-confidence generally, and as a pick-me-up if you are feeling low. You will need:

> **One silver candle**
> **One pink candle**
> **Lemon essential oil for anointing the pink candle**
> **Rosemary essential oil for anointing the silver candle**
> **New Moon**
> **A mirror**
> **Two empty jars**
> **Twelve small pieces of paper and a pen**

Place the mirror in front of you so that you can see yourself clearly. Put one jar next to the pink candle, and one next to the silver candle. Place the pieces of paper in easy reach. Cast your circle and light the candle. Looking into the mirror, chant three times:

> *I am the Goddess*
> *She is in me*
> *We are both beautiful*
> *So it is and so mote it be*

Now take the pen and paper, and write down on separate pieces of paper six things you feel unconfident about, or that you dislike about yourself. Start the sentence with I am or I have. Fold them over and put them in the jar next to the silver candle. Focus on the silver candle and say "I banish these thoughts" three times.

On the other six pieces of paper write down something you are proud of or like about yourself. Fold them over and put them in the jar next to the pink candle. Focus on the pink candle and say "I welcome these thoughts" three times. Thank the Goddess in your own words and close your circle.

Every night for the next six nights, cast your circle and light the candles. Take one piece of paper from each jar. Read out your negative comment, but instead of I am / I have ……. say I am not / I have not………. three times whilst focusing on the silver candle. Don't focus on the mirror as you read this. When you are finished, use the flame from the silver candle to burn the piece of paper, saying aloud "I banish this thought"

Take the positive comment, and looking into the mirror read it out loud three times, getting louder each time. Really feel the words. Concentrate on the pink candle flame and use it to burn the piece of paper, saying aloud "I welcome this thought." Spend some time meditating on the positive words, and when you are ready, thank the Goddess and close your circle.

Attract Love:

This spell will draw love into your life. It won't make one specific person fall in love with you, but it will bring the right match towards you. You will need:

A red candle
Jasmine oil to anoint the candle
Sweet almond oil or another suitable carrier oil
Full Moon
Pen and paper
Rose Quartz

Cast your circle and light the candle. With the pen and paper, write down the qualities that your ideal partner would have. They can be physical characteristics or personality traits. Write down everything you are looking for in an ideal partner. The list can be as long or short as you want, as long as you write down all the things that really matter to you.

Now take the rose quartz and holding it your hands, read the list out loud. Keeping hold of the rose quartz, think about how you will feel when you meet the person that has all of the characteristics you listed. Focus on the candle and visualise yourself happy and in a mutually loving relationship. Imagine the happiness you feel pouring from you and into the rose quartz. When you feel the rose quartz is charged, chant:

May this crystal like a beacon shine

To bring to me a love just mine

Two hearts in union joyfully

And it harm none, so mote it be

Fold the list of qualities in half, and then drip some of the candle wax onto it, folding it in half again to seal it. Thank the Goddess and close your circle. Place the list beneath your mattress, and keep the rose quartz crystal close to you in a pocket or bag until you find a suitable relationship, at which point you should bury them together somewhere safe.

Attract Luck:

This simple spell will make your days a little brighter by attracting more good luck, and deflecting bad luck. You will need:

> **A gold candle**
> **A black candle**
> **Bergamot oil to anoint the gold candle**
> **Frankincense oil to anoint the black candle**
> **New Moon**

Cast your circle and light the candles. Focus on the black candle flame and visualise all of your bad luck being burned away by the candle flame. As you visualise this, chant three times:

> *Bad luck is banished from my life*
> *No more struggle*
> *No more strife*
> *So mote it be*

Now focus on the gold candle flame and visualise good luck pouring in to your life. As you visualise this, chant three times:

> *Bring good things in life to me*
> *May I see each opportunity*
> *By the power of the moon*

My luck will be improving soon

So mote it be

Thank the Goddess and close the circle. Put the candles out, and repeat the ritual for three consecutive evenings, each time moving the black candle slightly further away from your body, and bringing the gold candle a little closer. This is to symbolise moving bad luck away from your life and bringing good luck into it.

New Job:

This spell is to be used when you have a job in mind to apply for, but before you have sent your application. Obviously, it also needs to be a job that your skills and experience meet the minimum requirements for. The spell is best performed on a full moon, but don't worry if there isn't a full moon before you have to send your application. If you can't do it on a full moon, the next best thing is to do the spell on a Monday. You will need:

> **A green candle**
> **Frankincense oil for anointing the candle**
> **The job details**
> **Your completed application or CV**

Cast your circle and light the candle. Focus on the candle flame and visualise yourself in the role. As you visualise this, chant:

> *This job is for me*
> *The employer will see*
> *My skills will shine through*
> *In the job interview*
> *So mote it be*

Repeat the chant until you feel a build-up of energy. When you feel this, pick up the application or CV and visualise all the energy flowing into the application until it glows a brilliant white. Thank the Goddess and close the circle. Let the candle burn down.

Post the application as soon as possible afterwards. If you are sending the job application electronically, use a printed copy of the application and keep it close to you when you send the electronic copy. As you send it, imagine some of the energy coming off the paper copy and travelling through cyberspace with your application. Leave the charged paper copy on or very close to your computer for a few days.

Attract Wealth:

Casting money spells can be a tricky business. The rituals themselves are not necessarily complicated, but the results can often be erratic or surprising. For example, casting a spell to 'get more money' may result in you landing a great job, winning the lottery, or gaining compensation due to a bad accident. Less drastically, you might get a pay rise and then find your household utility bills increase by the same amount. So how can you cast a spell to attract money without leaving yourself open to unfortunate ways of receiving that money?

We would all like more money, but what is driving you to cast a spell? What is the root cause of your financial need? Casting the spell out of greed rather than need is usually foolish. If you just want more money for the sake of it, then the spell is unlikely to work in a positive way, or at all. The spell below can help you attract wealth if you have a genuine need. You will need:

A green candle
Bergamot oil for anointing the candle
New Moon
A small piece of aventurine, or a coin (the highest denomination you can)

Cast your circle and light the candle. Focus on the candle flame and visualise your improved financial situation. Focus on your specific need, such as cupboards stocked with food or being able to pay all your essential bills in full each month. Spend some time focusing on the candle and meditating on achieving your aim, whilst holding the aventurine or coin. When it feels right chant three times:

Blessed Lady hear my plea
From money worries set me free
Send opportunity my way
To pay the bills I need to pay
And it harm none, so mote it be

Don't expect that money will just appear, but be on the look-out for opportunities to create wealth that might arise. Place the aventurine/coin in your wallet to help attract money to it.

Success:

This spell will boost your chances of success in achieving a goal. You will need:

>   **A green candle**
>   **Frankincense oil for anointing the candle**
>   **Full moon**
>   **Ground nutmeg**
>   **Pen and Paper**

Cast your circle and light the candle. Focus on the candle flame for a while and visualise achieving your goal. Imagine how you will feel, behave and look when you have achieved it. After a few minutes, take the pen and paper and write down your goal. Make it as clear and specific as you can, whilst remaining realistic. Sprinkle a pinch of nutmeg over the candle, and over the paper, chanting:

>   *I won't accept any less*
>   *Bring to me my own success*
>   *The goal I set I will achieve*
>   *And it harm none, so mote it be*

Take the paper that you wrote your goal on, and burn it with the candle flame. Close the circle and thank the Goddess. Let the candle burn down.

Increase Courage:

This spell will give you a boost of courage when you need to face something difficult. You will need:

A red candle
Clove oil for anointing the candle
Full Moon

Cast your circle and light the candle. Focus on the candle flame and take slow, deep breaths. Visualise with each breath out, you are releasing all of your fear and uncertainty. With each breath in you are breathing in renewed courage and faith in yourself. Do this until you feel calm and strong. Then chant this nine times, beginning quietly and increasing in volume each time:

Give me courage to endure
Whatever trials lay in store
I am strong and filled with might
By this sacred candle light
The fire of courage burns in me
And it harm none so mote it be

Close the circle and thank the Goddess. Let the candle burn down.

Protection:

This spell will help protect you from anybody who means you harm. You will need:

> **A white candle**
> **Rosemary oil for anointing the candle**
> **Waning Moon**

Cast your circle and light the candle. Focus on the candle flame and imagine the glow of the candle expanding to surround you in a protective glow. Within this protective shield you feel safe. Meditate on the safe and secure feeling of being within this protective shield. Chant three times:

> *Goddess wrap me in your arms*
> *And keep me safe from any harm*
> *No outside influence can hurt me*
> *And it harm none, so mote it be*

Close your circle, but continue to visualise the protective shield around you. Thank the Goddess. Let the candle burn down. Repeat the spell once a week if you continue to feel it is needed.

Simple Wish Spell:

This spell is a quick and simple way to ask for your wishes to be granted. This can be done at any moon phase, but a full moon is best. You will need:

> **A gold candle**
> **Basil oil for anointing the candle**
> **A bay leaf**
> **A marker pen**

Cast your circle and light the candle. Focus on the candle flame for a while and think about your wish. After a few minutes, take the bay leaf and marker pen and write down your wish on the bay leaf. Try and make it one word so that it can fit on the leaf.

Burn the bay leaf in the candle flame, whilst chanting:

> *Wish of mine*
> *Burning bright*
> *Bay leaf grant my wish tonight*
> *And it harm none, so mote it be*

Close the circle and thank the Goddess.

Ceromancy

Ceromancy is the practice of fortune telling using wax from a ritual candle. You will need:

A bowl of water
A candle (any colour, but white works very well)
Spoon
Towel

You can use any kind of candle for ceromancy, but as with other spells I find taper or pillar candles to be best. If your reading is about a relationship of any kind, you may want to use two candles. If you do use two candles, observe how the flame behaves. If one burns faster, it can mean that one person in the relationship is giving more.

Cast your circle and light the candle. Meditate on any questions you have for a few minutes. Hold the candle or candles above the bowl of water and let the wax drip into the bowl. When you are done, use the spoon to remove the hardened wax from the bowl and inspect the shapes. You should try and understand what the shapes mean to you personally, but if you are having a hard time deciphering them, here are some commonly accepted meanings for the shapes that sometimes result.

Airplane: A trip or a disappointment.
Anchor: Your loved one is faithful.
Ball: Your problem will roll away.
Bed: A restful holiday would be good for you.
Bells: A wedding.
Bird: News is coming.
Bridge: Time to take a chance.
Broom: Time to sweep in a change.
Candle: Spiritual growth.
Chain: Go ahead with your plans.
Circle: Time of reconciliation.
Cloud: Something or someone threatens you with a stormy situation.
Cross: You are protected.
Ear: Listen for opportunities to advance in your work.
Egg: There will soon be new developments.
Fan: A surprise is coming.
Feather: The problem will be solved.
Ghost: Someone from the past is looking for you.
Grass: Good fortune grows.
Heart: Friendship becomes love.

House: Better times are coming.

Leaf: There will soon be changes.

Lion: An unpleasant situation.

Moon: More money may be coming.

Mountain: Close friends are willing to help.

Pen: Letter from a friend or relative.

Ring: Marriage.

Scissors: Separation.

Snake: Beware a hidden threat.

Spider web: Pleasant occurrences.

Star: Happiness.

Sun: Good fortune.

Table: An abundance of blessings.

Tree: A good time for new ventures.

Walking Stick: Go and visit friends.

Wheel: Travel.

After the spell

So, you've cast your spell. What now? The first thing to remember is to be patient. Very few spells will work instantly, or even quickly. You also need to keep an open mind as the results of the spell may manifest in a way you weren't expecting. The most important thing is to back up your spells with simple action towards your goals. Spells can help breathe life into a plan of action, but you absolutely have to carry out the action. Casting the weight loss spell and then spending all your grocery money on cakes and fatty treats isn't going to help you, no matter how many spells you cast.

As you spend more time casting magic, you will begin to learn what works for you. It is a good idea to keep a diary specifically for your spell casting where you can note down which spell you used, any modifications you made, and the results you got. As you gain confidence in working magic, you can put your own spells together to achieve whatever outcome you would like. Creating your own spells is very powerful as it helps to focus your intention more fully. It can also be a lot of fun.

It may be that you want to create a spell that is 'darker' than the ones listed in this book. I have kept the details and spells in this book more in keeping with the 'light' side of magic because for beginners, this is what I feel is most appropriate to concentrate on. I won't pretend that there is no place in witchcraft for magic of a darker nature, but I would urge you to study thoroughly before you attempt to address anything darker. When most witches talk about darker magic we are not necessarily meaning an intention to harm anyone or break the Rede. Karma is something most witches believe in wholeheartedly. However, life, and witchcraft is about balance. As people we have positive traits, and negative traits. The Goddess reflects this in her darker aspects, and embracing these can be spiritually enlightening if you study them fully before attempting working with them.

    I'll close with the same sentiment I started with. With focus and the right intention you can cast a powerful spell using only a candle. Believe in your magic, and it will reward you three-fold. Good luck with your spells, and Blessed Be!

Printed in Poland
by Amazon Fulfillment
Poland Sp. z o.o., Wrocław